A FIRST LOOK AT DOGS

By Millicent E. Selsam and Joyce Hunt

ILLUSTRATED BY HARRIETT SPRINGER

WALKER AND COMPANY ✳ NEW YORK

A FIRST LOOK AT SERIES

A FIRST LOOK AT SNAKES, LIZARDS, AND OTHER REPTILES
A FIRST LOOK AT ANIMALS WITH BACKBONES
A FIRST LOOK AT BIRDS
A FIRST LOOK AT INSECTS
A FIRST LOOK AT WHALES
A FIRST LOOK AT MONKEYS AND APES
A FIRST LOOK AT ANIMALS WITHOUT BACKBONES
A FIRST LOOK AT FLOWERS
A FIRST LOOK AT THE WORLD OF PLANTS
A FIRST LOOK AT SHARKS
A FIRST LOOK AT CATS

Each of the nature books for this series is planned to develop the child's powers of observation and give him or her a rudimentary grasp of scientific classification.

For Tamar and Ariella

Thanks to Mr. James Doherty, Curator of Mammals, New York Zoological Society, for reading the text of this book.

Here is a dog.

Here is a cat.

Dogs and cats are the same in many ways.

Dogs and cats are *mammals* because
they have hair
and their babies nurse on the mother's milk.

Both dogs and cats belong to a group of mammals
called *Carnivora* (kar-*niv*-aw-ra).
Carnivores (*kar*-ni-vawrs) have powerful jaws
and sharp, pointed teeth that help them
catch animals and tear their flesh.

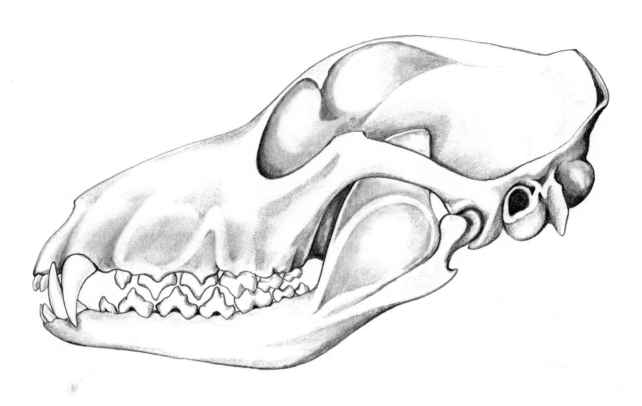

SKULL OF CARNIVORE

Although dogs and cats are the same in many ways, they are also different from each other.

DOGS

cannot pull claws back

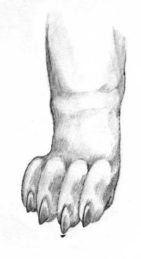

CATS

can pull claws back

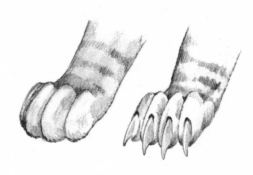

CLAWS IN   CLAWS OUT

long snouts (nose and jaws)

short snouts

DOGS

run after prey

CATS

stalk prey

bark or howl

meow or roar

9

Are these dogs?

WOLF

COYOTE

FOX

JACKAL

Wolves, coyotes (ki-*oh*-tees), foxes, and jackals
are all members of the dog family.
How do we tell one from another?

They can be told apart by their size.

Wolves are the largest members of the family.

Wolves usually run with their tails held straight out.

This animal looks like a wolf on stilts.
It is called a maned wolf because it has a mane
of long hair around its neck and shoulders.

Is this a wolf?

It looks like a wolf, but it is much smaller
and its snout is more pointed.
It is a coyote, sometimes called "little wolf."
A coyote usually runs with its tail held down
between its hind legs.

Remember how the wolf runs.

Foxes are even smaller than coyotes.
Their legs are much shorter too.
You cannot always tell foxes apart by their color.
But they can be told apart by their markings.

Find the fox with a dark stripe down its tail.

Find the fox with a white tail tip and dark feet.

Find the fox with a dark tail tip.

RED FOX

Sometimes the red fox is black, grey, or of mixed colors.

This is the smallest of the foxes.

KIT FOX

GRAY FOX

This is the only fox that can climb trees.

17

This fox has small round ears
and the bottoms of its feet are furry.
It looks like a little polar bear.
It is an Arctic fox.
It is all white only in the winter.
At other times it can be brown or gray.

Somewhere below these two big ears is a little pale face.
This animal is called a fennec (*fen*-nick).
It is the smallest member of the dog family.

Jackals live in the warmer parts of the world.
They look like coyotes but they are smaller.

COMMON JACKAL

Some jackals can be told apart by their markings.
Match the jackal to its name.
Side-striped jackal.
Black-backed jackal.

21

Here are some other members of the dog family.
Which has a "mask" on its face?
Which looks more like a baby pig than a dog?
Which has round ears and
dark and light blotches all over its body?

CAPE HUNTING DOG

RACCOON DOG

BUSH DOG

23

TAME DOGS

Thousands of years ago, when people lived in caves,
the wolf was trained to help them hunt and protect them.
Little by little the wolf was tamed (domesticated).

All the different kinds of tame dogs we know today
from the toy poodle to the Great Dane
came from this once-wild animal.

Dogs are put into different groups according to the way they are used, not by their shape, size, or markings. These groups are called *breeds*.

SPORTING DOGS

Setters, spaniels, and retrievers (ri-*tree*-vurs) may look very different but they are all in the sporting dog group because they are trained to hunt birds.

Setters "point" at the birds.

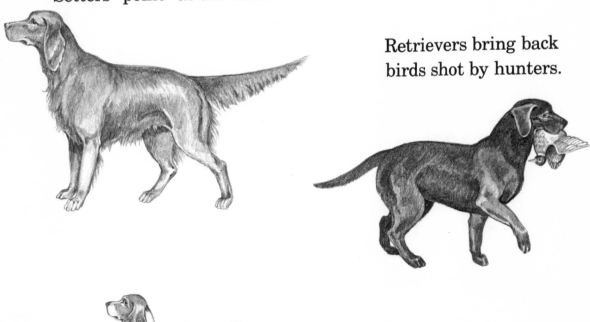

Retrievers bring back birds shot by hunters.

Spaniels "flush" birds out of their hiding places.

HOUNDS

Hounds are dogs that track rabbits,
squirrels, raccoons and other small animals.

Some hound dogs track by using their noses.

BLOODHOUND

Other hound dogs hunt by sight.

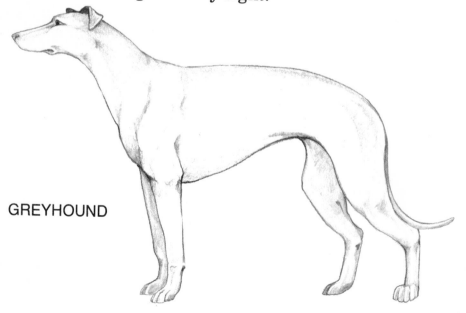

GREYHOUND

TERRIERS

Terriers also help hunters.

They chase and find small animals, even those that have hiding places underground.

Which terrier has a head like a box and long legs?

Which terrier has a head like a box and short legs?

Which terrier looks like a lamb?

BEDLINGTON TERRIER

AIRDALE TERRIER

SCOTCH TERRIER

WORKING DOGS

All the dogs on this page work.

The Doberman guards houses.

The collie herds sheep.

The German shepherd
leads blind people.

TOY DOGS

Toy dogs are tiny.
Find the dog with a pushed-in face and curly tail.
Find the dog that looks like a ball of fur
with a fox-like face.
Find the dog that looks like a mop.

POMERANIAN

PUG

MALTESE

29

NONSPORTING DOGS

All dogs that are not sporting dogs, or
hounds, or terriers, or working dogs,
or toy dogs, are called nonsporting dogs.

DALMATIAN

STANDARD POODLE

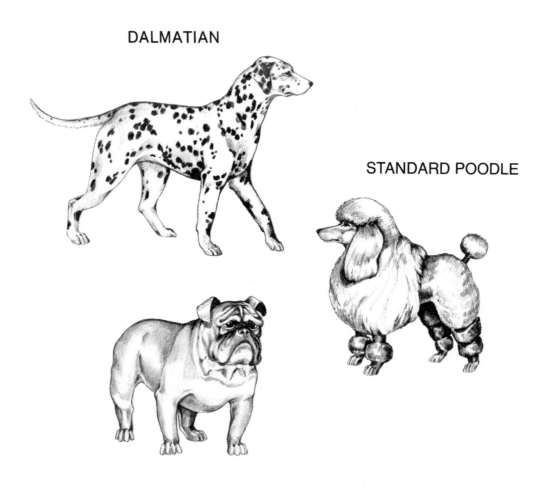

ENGLISH BULLDOG

THE MUTTS

When two different breeds of dogs mate,
the puppies may look like the mother, the father,
or they may look like a mixture of both.
They are called *mutts*.

TO TELL MEMBERS OF THE DOG FAMILY APART

Look at the size and the way they hold their tails.

WOLF

COYOTE

Look at the markings.

GRAY FOX

CAPE HUNTING DOG

TO TELL TAME DOGS APART, YOU MUST KNOW HOW THEY ARE USED.

See if you remember in what group these dogs belong.

BLOODHOUND

IRISH SETTER

SCOTCH TERRIER

COLLIE

PUG

DALMATIAN